I Am an Orthodox Jew

by Laura Greene
illustrated by Lisa C. Wesson

Holt, Rinehart and Winston
New York

Library of Congress Cataloging in Publication Data
Greene, Laura.   I Am an Orthodox Jew.
1. Jewish way of life—Juvenile literature.
2. Orthodox Judaism—Juvenile literature.
I. Wesson, Lisa. II. Title.
BM107.G73   296.7   78-14094
ISBN 0-03-044661-9

9-89

For reading and commenting on the manuscript, thanks to:

Mira Fraenkel, Educational Consultant
    Milwaukee Board of Jewish Education

Elaine Sanderson, Librarian at Hillel Academy
    and Milwaukee Board of Jewish Education

Rabbi Harry B. Pastor, Congregation Shalom
    Milwaukee, Wisconsin

Thanks also to my friends at the Lubavitch house
    and teachers and students at Hillel,
        but special thanks to my editor, Miriam Chaikin.

Book sto

To Victor
All my love, all my life   L.G.

With gratitude to Miriam Chaikin   L.C.W.

My name is Aaron Katz and I am an Orthodox Jew. I go to a Hebrew Day School. A big yellow bus stops in front of my house each morning. I run out the side door and race my sister Rachel to the bus. We don't want to be late.

In my school every boy wears a little hat. It is called a kippa. It is also called a yarmulke. I wear a kippa at home, too. So do my father and brothers. We wear them all the time. My father says the kippa is a sign of respect for God and our way of life. He says it is a symbol of the separation between man and God.

I wear tzitzit all the time, too. Tzitzit are the fringes on the special, four-cornered garment which I wear under my clothes. The Hebrew Bible says I must wear them. It says that when I look at the fringes I will remember to do God's commandments, but sometimes I forget, even when I see my tzitzit.

I go to a Hebrew Day School instead of a public school because my parents want me to learn lots of Jewish things. They also want me to know Hebrew as well as I know English.

In school, half the day we learn in English. We study the same things you do and even have some of the same books. The other half of the day we learn in Hebrew and study the Hebrew Bible. We learn about the history, customs, and laws of the Jewish people.

Andy, my best friend, isn't Jewish. He goes to a public school.

Once Andy slept at my house. We had fun. We had hamburgers, peas, and french fries for supper. When Andy invited me to sleep at his house, I brought my own food, but he gave me an orange to eat. At his house I may eat fruit that can be peeled. I am not permitted to eat food prepared in his kitchen. I eat only kosher food prepared in a kosher kitchen.

Sometimes I wish I could eat Andy's food or go out for a hamburger like some other kids, but very few restaurants serve kosher food prepared according to Orthodox law, and this is the only kind of food I may eat.

But there are lots of other things I can do together with my friends.

On Fridays the children in my school are dismissed early. We want to prepare for the Sabbath. We want to be home before the sun sets and the Sabbath begins.

In winter the sun sets very early, so I am home soon after lunch. As the sun is about to set, my mother gives Rachel coins to put in our tzedakah—or charity—box. I can hear them clink against the other coins. When the box is full, it will be Rachel's turn to decide which charity will receive the money. I think she should choose Israel, the way I did last time. But she says she wants to choose the children's hospital around the corner.

I think about how I can make her change her mind, and I watch my mother strike a match and light the Sabbath candles. Two candles would be enough, but she lights six, one for each member of our family.

She looks pretty with the Sabbath scarf on her head. It used to be my grand-mother's. Someday it will be my sister's. Sometimes my mother and sister say the candle blessing together. I listen. My mother kisses us on the eyes after she says it.

Soon my father and brothers come home from the synagogue. They always go to the synagogue before dinner on Fridays. Sometimes I go with them, but my mother and sister usually stay at home to prepare for the Sabbath.

When my father comes home he places his hand on my head and blesses me. Then he blesses my brothers. He calls to my sister and blesses her also. But when he says to her, "May you be like Sarah, Rebekah, Rachel, and Leah," we giggle. It's a silly blessing. She already is Rachel.

We sing songs to welcome the Sabbath. Then at last we are ready to eat. But we must first wash our hands. We must always wash our hands and say a blessing before eating bread.

At the table my father says the blessing

over the wine and then over the hallah, the Sabbath bread. My brothers and I had to learn these blessings because we are boys. My sister learned them just because she wanted to. It was easy. She hears them every Friday night.

After dinner we sing more songs. My mother has a sweet voice. My father and I sing off key. The rest of the evening we read or tell stories or play games. We enjoy ourselves until bedtime.

On Saturday mornings Rachel and my mother often decide to go to the synagogue with my father, my brothers, and me. In our synagogue the women sit in a balcony separate from the men. This is because the men are supposed to think only about their prayers and not have any outside thoughts. Rachel does not like this rule. She says she cannot see the Rabbi as well as I can. She cannot hear very well either. That makes her angry.

While the men are praying, the children walk in and out during the service. We see people we know and talk to them. We play in the halls and at our seats. Sometimes we talk. No one minds.

Up front the men are very serious. Sometimes they shake hands. My father told me that they are congratulating one another on how well they read from the holy scroll.

I know how to read Hebrew, too, and some day I will be called to read from the Torah. That will be at my bar mitzvah. My bar mitzvah is a very important occasion.

It is the day I am accepted as a man among Jews. It is the day I am given the honor to read from the Torah before the entire congregation. I will be thirteen years old when this happens.

My sister will never have this great honor because she is a girl. She doesn't think that's fair because she reads Hebrew, too.

After services we walk home and have a big dinner. My mother and sister prepared the dinner Friday before the Sabbath began. The food is kept warm all night so that they do not have to cook on the Sab-

bath. Cooking is work, and working is not permitted on the Sabbath. We have company for the Sabbath meal. The food is delicious. I like the Sabbath because everything about it is special.

After dinner my sister goes to play at the house of her friend Ellen. Andy comes to my house. We have our third Sabbath

meal, a very little one, just before the day ends. When there are three stars in the sky the Sabbath is over. Rachel comes home for the Havdalah service.

My father lets Andy hold the braided candle. Then he says the blessings. He lets us all smell the spices in the spice box. Tonight it is a mixture of cinnamon and nutmeg. All of the senses—taste, smell, sight, touch, sound—must be pleased during the Sabbath, and this is the way we

please the sense of smell. It is like a feast
to our noses. We will remember the smell,
and then we will not be sad that we must
wait a whole week for another Sabbath,
another special day.

My father puts the candle out by dipping the flame into a dish of wine. Then he winks at Andy, takes a tiny drop of wine, and puts it into Andy's pocket for good

luck. He does it to Rachel and me, too. We know that this is just a superstition, but it is fun to believe that the wine will make us rich.

A new week begins with the coming of night. Andy, Rachel, and I go outside. Ellen is waiting for us. We play a game together.